Courageous Heroes of the American West

Daniel Boone
Courageous Frontiersman

William R. Sanford and Carl R. Green

Enslow Publishers, Inc.
40 Industrial Road
Box 398
Berkeley Heights, NJ 07922
USA
http://www.enslow.com

Original edition published as *Daniel Boone: Wilderness Pioneer* in 1997.

Library of Congress Cataloging-in-Publication Data

Sanford, William R. (William Reynolds), 1927–

    Daniel Boone : courageous frontiersman / William R. Sanford and Carl R. Green.

       p. cm. — (Courageous heroes of the American West)

    Original edition published as Daniel Boone : Wilderness Pioneer in 1997.

    With unupdated bibliography.

    Includes index.

    Summary: "Discusses the life of Daniel Boone, the scout, hunter, and frontier hero, who
created the Wilderness Road to open up Kentucky to settlement and became a legend in
American history"—Provided by publisher.

    ISBN 978-0-7660-4002-1

    1. Boone, Daniel, 1734–1820—Juvenile literature. 2. Pioneers—Kentucky—Biography—
Juvenile literature. 3. Kentucky—Biography—Juvenile literature. 4. Frontier and pioneer
life—Kentucky—Juvenile literature. I. Green, Carl R. II. Title.

    F454.B66S26 2012

    976.9'02092—dc23

    [B]

                           2011037736

Future editions:

Paperback ISBN 978-1-4644-0085-8

ePUB ISBN 978-1-4645-0992-6

PDF ISBN 978-1-4646-0992-3

Printed in the United States of America

032012 Lake Book Manufacturing, Inc., Melrose Park, IL

10 9 8 7 6 5 4 3 2 1

To Our Readers: We have done our best to make sure all Internet addresses in this book were
active and appropriate when we went to press. However, the author and the Publisher have no
control over, and assume no liability for, the material available on those Internet sites or on other
Web sites they may link to. Any comments or suggestions can be sent by e-mail to comments@
enslow.com or to the address on the back cover.

♻ Enslow Publishers, Inc., is committed to printing our books on recycled paper. The paper in
every book contains 10% to 30% post-consumer waste (PCW). The cover board on the outside of
each book contains 100% PCW. Our goal is to do our part to help young people and the
environment too!

Illustration Credits: © 2012 Clipart.com, a division of Getty Images, pp. 24, 28, 38; *Daniel
Boone, the pioneer of Kentucky. A biography*, © 1866 (p. 160), p. 30; Enslow Publishers, Inc.,
p. 19; © Enslow Publishers, Inc. / Paul Daly, p. 1; Everett Collection, p. 43; The Granger
Collection, NYC, p. 34; Library of Congress Prints and Photographs, pp. 7, 15; *Life of Daniel
Boone* © 1856, frontispiece, p. 11; National Archives and Records Administration, p. 41;
National Park Service, painting by David Wright, p. 20.

Cover Illustration: © Enslow Publishers, Inc / Paul Daly.

Contents

Authors' Note

For more than a hundred years, the lands west of the Appalachians lay beyond the reach of America's early colonists. The original thirteen colonies held fast to the Atlantic coast. Strict laws, rugged mountains, and fierce American Indian tribes blocked movement beyond the Appalachians. Only trappers and traders ventured into what was then the colonies' Wild West. Daniel Boone helped break the barriers by opening Kentucky to settlement. This is the true story of how one strong-willed woodsman helped tame a wild and rugged frontier.

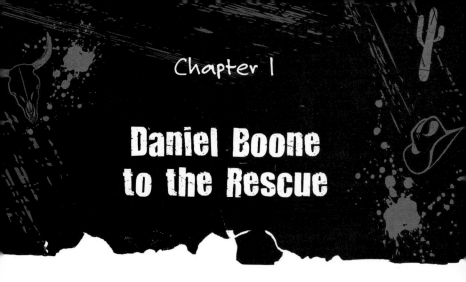

Chapter 1

Daniel Boone to the Rescue

In July 1776, the American colonies were focused on gaining their freedom. Patriots clashed with British redcoats in battles all along the East Coast. In the wilds of Kentucky, settlers faced a different foe. The Cherokee and Shawnee were determined to evict the white man from their hunting grounds.

Daniel Boone's settlement at Boonesborough was a prime target. However, a string of calm summer days gave a false sense of peace. On Sunday, July 7, three teenage girls slipped away to go canoeing. Daniel's thirteen-year-old daughter, Jemima, handled the steering. Betsey and Fanny Callaway did the paddling. Back at the settlement, Daniel was taking a nap.

On the far side of the river, a Cherokee chief named Hanging Maw kept watch. Little by little, the current swept the girls' canoe closer to the shore. Suddenly, a Shawnee warrior jumped in and held it fast.

The girls screamed. Fanny, a tiny thirteen-year-old, hit out with her paddle. Betsey, the oldest of the trio at sixteen, joined in. More warriors jumped into the fray. They yanked the paddles away and dragged the girls into the woods. The screaming finally stopped when a Shawnee threatened to take Betsey's scalp.

Like her father, Jemima was a quick thinker. Pointing to a cut on one bare foot, she told Hanging Maw she could not walk another step. Fanny, too, was barefoot. Hanging Maw told his men to give the two some moccasins. Next, the braves cut off the girls' long dresses at the knees. They did not want their escape to be slowed by skirts catching in the brambles.

Back at Boonesborough, the screams had aroused the settlement. Daniel ran barefoot to the riverbank. For the moment, pursuit was delayed. The only canoe lay on the far side of the river. Twelve-year-old John Gass swam across to retrieve it.

Once he had crossed the river, the trail was easy to follow. The girls had dropped bits of cloth and twigs as they trudged along. While Daniel studied the signs, Richard Callaway and a party of horsemen joined him. The riders were eager to chase after the kidnappers. Daniel shook his head. The Shawnee, he said, would kill the girls the moment they heard hoofbeats.

In July 1776, Daniel Boone's daughter Jemima was kidnapped by the Shawnee in the Kentucky wilderness. In this dramatized illustration, Boone rescues his daughter from the raiding party.

Callaway agreed that Daniel was right. He and his men struck out for the Licking River to lay an ambush. In camp that night, Daniel saw that his men were not equipped for a long chase. He sent young Gass back to Boonesborough for buckskins, food, powder, and shot—and Daniel's moccasins.

By Tuesday, Hanging Maw was forty miles from the river. He was sure he was safe. His warriors killed a buffalo and stopped to cook the meat. They did not know that Daniel had outguessed them. As the Shawnee prepared their meal, the rescue party closed in.

The woodsmen were thirty yards away when a lookout spotted them. The men opened fire at once. The Shawnee fled, too startled to think of harming the girls. Daniel fired and saw one of the Shawnee go down. "Run, gals, run!" the men yelled.

A tomahawk whizzed by Betsey's head. A moment later, one of the rescuers mistook her for a Shawnee. He was about to hit her with his rifle butt when Daniel grabbed his arm. "Don't kill her when we've traveled so far to save her," Daniel yelled. A moment later, Jemima was safe in his arms.

A month later, the people of Boonesborough gathered to celebrate Betsey's marriage. Daniel had blazed the trail into Kentucky only one year earlier. Now he was an honored guest at the settlement's first wedding.

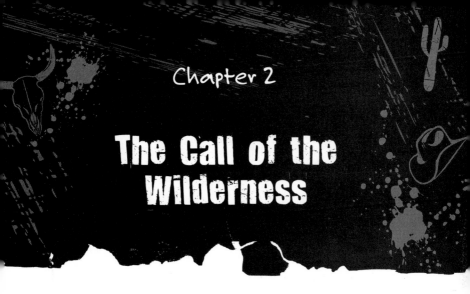

Chapter 2

The Call of the Wilderness

Daniel Boone's love of the wilderness was inborn. His grandfather, George Boone, brought the family to America in 1717. From his home in western England, Boone had heard about William Penn's colony. Like Penn, Boone was a member of the Society of Friends—the Quakers. Pennsylvania, reports said, offered cheap land and religious freedom.

At first, the Boones settled twelve miles north of Philadelphia. Within a short time, they were on the move again. As historian John Bakeless writes: "The Boones were wanderers born. They had the itching foot. . . . They heard of distant lands and knew that they must go there." George Boone's first move took him only a few miles. In 1718, he settled on four hundred acres in Oley Township. The town of Reading grew up nearby.

Boone's son Squire married Sarah Morgan in 1720. Squire was a weaver, but he also hungered to own land. By 1730, he was farming almost four hundred acres of land in Oley. There, on November 2, 1734, Sarah gave birth to her sixth child. The Boones called him Daniel, after Sarah's brother.

The Boone farm lay at the edge of the wilderness. American Indian hunters were frequent visitors. Young Daniel made friends with them. Unlike most boys of his time, he studied the American Indian's way of life. Those early lessons paid off later. Daniel's ability to think like an Indian saved his life more than once.

When Daniel was six, smallpox struck the township. Sarah kept her children at home, hoping they could avoid the dreaded disease. According to one old story, the confinement did not please young Daniel. The answer, he thought, was to catch smallpox. Once he recovered, he again would be free to wander. One night, he sneaked off to a neighbor's farm. There, he crawled into bed with a child who was blotched with smallpox sores. As he had planned, the same blotches soon showed up on his skin. Luckily, he and the other Boone children survived the outbreak.

When Daniel was ten, his father bought twenty-five acres of wooded pasture. The land lay some miles

As a child, Daniel Boone learned to hunt with a throwing stick. At age thirteen, his father gave him a rifle. Daniel would stay in the forests hunting, sometimes for days, before returning home.

from the main farm. Daniel spent the next six summers there with his mother. Their job was to tend the Boones' cattle. Squire stayed home to manage his looms and his blacksmith shop. Daniel's oldest sister cared for the younger children.

By day, Daniel roamed the woods as the cattle grazed. At night, he drove them home for milking. The boy also helped feed the family. He knew how to find nuts and berries, but hunting was his real passion. Too young to carry a gun, Daniel relied on a throwing stick. Before long, he could kill a rabbit at ten yards. His father gave him a short-barreled, muzzle-loading rifle when Daniel was thirteen. Gifted with a keen eye, the young woodsman soon became a top marksman.

The Boones' cows sometimes had to find their own way home. When hunting was good, Daniel stayed away for days at a time. Sarah worried about him, with good reason. American Indian hunters prowled those same woods. The danger excited Daniel. He learned to move through the woods as silently as a shadow. The woods became his schoolroom. Each sight, sound, and smell told him its story.

Daniel never did have much real schooling. Late in life, he told his children that he had never gone to school. A sister-in-law, Sarah Day Boone, taught him to read and write. Years later, a son-in-law polished his skills a little. Despite those efforts, Daniel often spelled words the way they sounded. *Copied* became "coppyed." *All right* came out "awl wright." *Business* turned into "bisness."

When his Uncle John complained, Squire had a ready answer. "Let the girls do the spelling and Daniel will do the shooting."

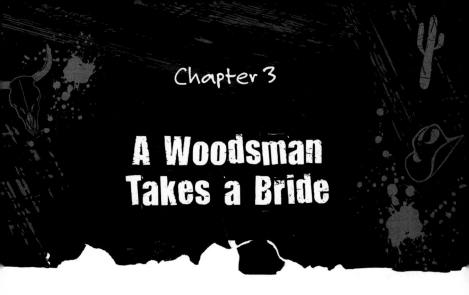

Chapter 3

A Woodsman Takes a Bride

In 1748, the local Quakers expelled Squire Boone. His crime? Two of his children had married non-Quakers. Two years later, Squire led his family south to North Carolina. He bought 640 acres near the Yadkin River. Land was cheap on the frontier.

The Boones cleared their fields and planted a corn crop. Daniel hunted deer, turkey, and bear with Tick Licker, his long-barreled flintlock. Legend tells us he could shoot a tick off a bear's snout at one hundred yards. Soon, he was staying in the woods for weeks at a time. On the frontier, this was known as a "long hunt." The hides and furs he brought back sold for a good price. After one hunt, the teenager spent all his profits "on a general jamboree."

In 1754, British and French forces clashed on the western frontier. The first shots signaled the start of the French and Indian War. In 1755, the British sent General Edward Braddock to seize Fort Duquesne from the French. Daniel went along as a wagon driver. He enjoyed the trek through western Pennsylvania. At night, he listened spellbound to John Finley's yarns about far-off Kentucky. Finley told him that the land beyond the Appalachians was a paradise.

On July 9, Braddock's troops ran into an ambush. French soldiers, fighting beside Iroquois and Shawnee warriors, cut down the advance guard. As war cries echoed in their ears, the British redcoats panicked and fled. Daniel's wagon was caught in the crush. Unable to turn, he jumped on his lead horse and cut the reins. Then he rode for his life.

Soon after he returned home, Daniel met the love of his life. He first saw Rebecca Bryan at a wedding, but legend tells a more romantic tale. Daniel was hunting deer at night, the story goes. All at once, he saw the light of a friend's torch reflected in a pair of startled eyes. As Daniel raised his rifle, a sixth sense told him to hold his fire. In the next instant, Rebecca jumped up and ran off through the woods.

Daniel must have chased after her, for he married Rebecca on August 14, 1756. She was seventeen years old, an attractive girl with black hair and dark eyes.

The groom was twenty-one. He stood five feet, eight inches tall, with broad shoulders and chest. Piercing blue eyes studied the world from beneath a mop of dark hair. Thin lips framed a large, mobile mouth. His Cherokee friends called him Wide Mouth.

The newlyweds moved into a snug cabin on Sugar Creek. Rebecca proved to be an able helpmate. When Daniel went hunting, she took over the farmwork. In time, she would also give birth to six sons and four daughters. Their first child, James, was born in 1757.

This illustration depicts General Braddock's defeat during the French and Indian War in 1755. Daniel Boone barely escaped the ambush. After his wagon was destroyed during the British retreat, he cut his lead horse loose and rode it to safety.

For ten years, the Boones lived a quiet life. Daniel raised crops on a 640-acre farm. In the fall and early winter, he left for his long hunts. One hunting trip in 1760 took him into eastern Tennessee. Years later, someone found a beech tree there with deeply inscribed letters. The carving read: *D. Boon cilled a Bar on tree in the year 1760*. Some argue that it is a fake. Daniel, they say, never misspelled his own name.

By the mid-1760s, Daniel was growing restless. Game was growing scarce as settlers flooded into the Yadkin Valley. In 1765, he trekked to Florida to check out Spain's offer of free land. The hunting was poor, and the swamps bred swarms of insects. Despite these drawbacks, Daniel talked to Rebecca about moving. She refused to leave her family and friends.

In 1769, John Finley stopped by the Boone cabin. Daniel had not forgotten his friend's stories of Kentucky. Now he wanted to see the paradise for himself. On May 1, Daniel led Finley and four friends westward. The men passed through the Cumberland Gap on an American Indian trail called the Warrior's Trace. A few weeks later, Daniel stood on a hilltop north of the Kentucky River. There he gazed for the first time at "the beautiful [land] of Kentucke."

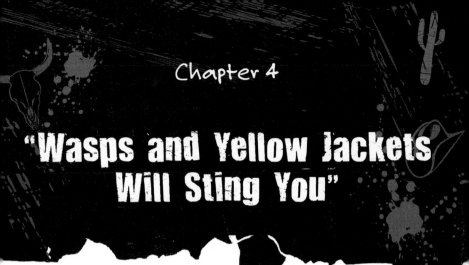

Chapter 4

"Wasps and Yellow Jackets Will Sting You"

The name Kentucky came from the Iroquois word for meadows, *kanta-ke*. Daniel Boone was not the first to glimpse the land's bluegrass meadows. The Shawnee, Cherokee, and other American Indian tribes hunted there. English and French traders had crisscrossed the region for decades.

For six months, Daniel's party hunted deer and trapped beaver. All was well until the day a Shawnee war party cornered Daniel and his brother-in-law, John Stewart. The Shawnee soon released their captives, but they took all the skins and horses. With them went the profits of six months labor.

The Shawnee leader warned, "If you are so foolish as to venture here again . . . the wasps and yellow jackets will sting you severely."

The two hunters ignored the threat. For several days, they tracked the war party. Then, while the

Shawnee slept, they stole back their horses. A day later, the Shawnee recaptured them. The warriors seemed to enjoy the game. One of them tied a horse collar around Daniel's neck. Then the Shawnee ordered him to dance. When the warriors stopped laughing, they took their captives with them.

A week later, the party camped near the Ohio River. That night, Daniel and John broke loose. Moving swiftly, they grabbed two rifles and hid in a canebrake. The Shawnee let them go. They were in a rush to get home with their loot.

By this time, Finley and the others had fled. Daniel and John went back to trapping. Daniel's brother Squire helped by showing up with fresh supplies. A month later, John failed to keep a rendezvous. Daniel searched for him but found only the letters *JS* carved on a tree. Five years later, a hunter found a skeleton inside a hollow tree. The body could well have been that of John Stewart. Wounded by Shawnee, he may have bled to death in his hiding place.

In May 1770, Squire left to take a load of hides and furs to market. For two months, Daniel ranged across Kentucky on his own. Day by day, he added to his mental map of the land. The map told him the location of each hill, stream, and salt lick. When he felt lonely,

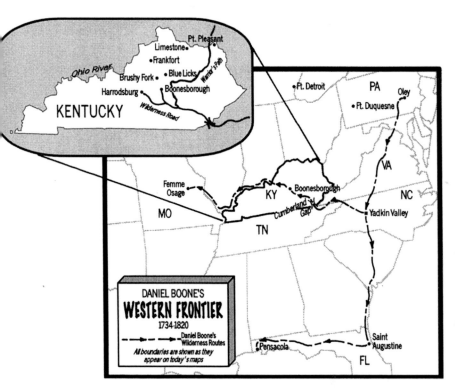

In May 1770, Daniel Boone traveled across Kentucky alone for two months. As he walked, he created a mental map of the region's rivers, hills, and other important landmarks. This is a map of Boone's Western frontier.

Daniel sang songs and talked to himself. In July, he met Squire at their old camp.

The pair finally headed for home in March 1771. Along the way, they ran into more bad luck. A band of Cherokee raiders stole their furs, horses, and rifles. For two years, Daniel wrote, he had not tasted salt, sugar, or bread. Now he returned to the Yadkin Valley empty-handed and in debt. He had paid for his supplies and equipment with borrowed money.

Daniel Boone leads a column of settlers through the Cumberland Gap. During the long and difficult journey, the party had to fend off attacks from the Delaware, Shawnee, and Cherokee.

All this time, Americans were pushing beyond the mountains. A British law had forbidden this movement, however, it could not be enforced. In 1773, a wealthy Virginia landowner named William Russell caught the Kentucky fever. He picked Daniel to lead his expedition.

Rebecca gave birth to their eighth child that spring. A few months later, the whole Boone family set out for Kentucky. A number of Boones and Bryans joined the party. Each group took only what could be carried on packhorses. Small children rode in baskets tied to the saddles.

The party made slow progress. Daniel had to send back for more supplies. His sixteen-year-old son, James, rode with the supply train. On October 9, a Delaware war party fired on the group as the men lay sleeping. The first shots killed two men and wounded James Boone and Henry Russell. The warriors then stormed into the camp and tortured the helpless teenagers. The two boys died slow and painful deaths.

The settlers lost heart when they learned of the four deaths. Daniel buried his son and returned home, where his fields lay untended. To feed his family, he hunted all through the winter. In the spring, he returned to Kentucky to visit his son's grave.

The killings sparked a brief, bloody war. After white riflemen killed a number of blameless American Indians, Shawnee and Cherokee warriors struck back. Daniel, now a militia lieutenant, took charge of several frontier forts. The people who took shelter there trusted his leadership. By the time the fighting ended in the fall, he had risen to the rank of captain.

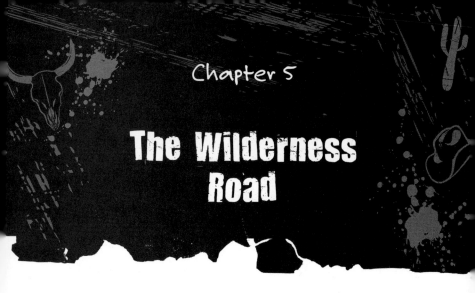

Chapter 5

The Wilderness Road

When Daniel was unable to repay his debts, the lenders took him to court. To defend himself, he turned to lawyer Richard Henderson. When they met, Daniel often described Kentucky's wonders to the wealthy North Carolinian.

Henderson listened carefully. In 1775, he formed the Transylvania Company as a way of speculating in western lands. Before he could do so, he had to gain title to the land. The lawyer's solution was to open talks with the Cherokee. The fact that the tribe did not own the land did not stop him. Neither did the fact that he was breaking the law. Since 1763, settlers had been confined to the lands east of the Appalachians.

It was Daniel who arranged the meeting. More than a thousand Cherokee gathered in March 1775 for the talks. Henderson won their good will by showing up with six wagons full of trade goods. He claimed that the cargo was worth $50,000. Some observers did not believe him. They saw mostly "cheap trinkets," firearms, and rum.

After much debate, the Cherokee sold 20 million acres. The land lay between the Kentucky and Cumberland rivers. Henderson also won the right to open a road to his land. Most of the Cherokee leaders signed the Great Grant. One who did not was a chief named Dragging Canoe. "Brother, we have given you a fine land," he warned Daniel. "But . . . you will have much trouble in settling it."

Daniel left the meeting early. Henderson had offered him two thousand acres of prime wilderness land. In payment, Daniel had promised to open a road into Kentucky. His friends and neighbors hurried to join him. The pay was good—ten British pounds (£10) to each workman. As a bonus, they were allowed to take the best land for themselves.

The road builders met on the Virginia-North Carolina border. Squire was there. So was Daniel's daughter Susannah and her new husband. Fourteen-year-old Susannah had hired on to cook and keep camp. It was a good time for Daniel to be away from home. In mid-April, a creditor swore out a warrant for

Daniel Boone led a crew of workers who were hired to open the Wilderness Road into Kentucky. The expedition chopped down trees, cleared brush, and dug out stones to open a route through the dense forest.

his arrest. The sheriff did his best, but he could not find Daniel. Across the court papers he scrawled, "Gone to Kentucky."

Daniel marked the way along the Warrior's Trace. The woodsmen felled the first trees on March 10, 1775. Yard by yard, the men carved a pack trail through the wilderness. They cleared brush and dug out rocks. They slashed their way through canebrakes. Snow and sleet slowed the work but did not stop it. Henderson later wrote that "no part of the road [was] tolerable." Most of what became known as the Wilderness Road was hilly, stony, or muddy.

Two weeks of backbreaking labor took the crew into Kentucky. Certain that the worst was over, the workers camped near a boiling spring. On March 24, they awoke to the sound of gunfire. Dragging Canoe's prophecy was coming true. As Daniel described it, "A party of Indians fired on my company about half an hour before day. [They] killed Mr. Twetty and his negro." A second attack two days later cost two more lives.

Only Daniel's cool courage kept the men from fleeing. On April 6, the weary party finally reached journey's end. Daniel led the workers to a site on the south bank of the Kentucky River. There, they built a cluster of log huts. A crude, unfinished twelve-foot stockade guarded the enclosure. The men called it Fort Boone.

Daniel resolved to bring his family to Kentucky. He felt sure his tiny settlement would grow. His workers, too, were pleased with their prospects. Indeed, their hunger for land caused a serious problem. The men often left the fort unguarded while they scrambled to stake their claims.

Henderson's caravan of packhorses arrived two weeks later. With them came seeds, trade goods, black powder, and cattle. Henderson renamed the site Boonesborough. He later wrote: "It was owing to Boone's confidence in us and the people's in him that a stand was ever attempted."

Chapter 6

Running the Gauntlet

The first shots of the American Revolution rang out on April 19, 1775. In Kentucky, the settlers cheered the news. Then they turned back to their own problems.

The Transylvania Company refused to allow free elections. Worse still, it planned to charge settlers a yearly rent for each acre farmed. Daniel also worried about the lack of game. He pushed for a rule to keep hunters from killing for sport.

Back East, the company met more setbacks. The Continental Congress refused to make Kentucky the fourteenth colony. Virginia, in turn, declared that Kentucky was one of its counties. The company was forced to focus on other land grants. It never did give Daniel all of the acres he had been promised.

In September, Daniel led a second pack train to Boonesborough. Rebecca and seven of their children

In 1775, Daniel Boone led a second group of settlers, including Rebecca and seven of his children, to Boonesborough.

were at his side. The hardships of frontier life waited for the newcomers. Food was scarce. The crude cabins were damp and drafty. The Shawnee were on the warpath. Even so, the pack trains kept coming. More than five hundred settlers now lived in Kentucky.

In August 1776, a rider brought good news: the Declaration of Independence had been signed. Anxious to put down the rebellion, the British struck back. Their agents urged the Shawnee to mount new raids. The threat sent settlers running for safety. By year's end, only 150 riflemen remained in all of Kentucky.

In April 1777, a war party caught twelve settlers outside the fort. Daniel was one of them. "Boys, we have to fight!" Daniel yelled. "Sell your lives as dear as possible!"

Daniel led a charge through the band of Shawnee. Just as a path opened, a rifle ball shattered his ankle. As Daniel fell, a Shawnee jumped on him. Simon Kenton shot the warrior and crushed a second Shawnee's skull with his gun barrel. Then he hoisted Daniel to his shoulders and ran for the fort. The Shawnee withdrew when the gates slammed shut.

By January 1778, the salt used for preserving food was running low. Daniel, his ankle well healed, led thirty men to the spring at Blue Licks. There, the other men made salt by boiling the briny water in iron kettles. Daniel took care of the hunting.

On February 7, four Shawnee captured Daniel during a snowstorm. Back at the Shawnee camp, Daniel saw the size of the war party and shivered. Boonesborough surely would fall if the Shawnee attacked. So he hit on a plan to trade the salt-boiling party for the safety of those at the fort. The lure of an easy victory appealed to Blackfish, the Shawnee chief. He knew the British would pay £20 for each captive.

When Daniel Boone escaped from the Shawnee in 1778, he had to travel 160 miles to reach Boonesborough. His appearance had changed so much by the time he reached the settlement that his friends could scarcely recognize him.

A day later, Daniel approached his men and explained his plan. They agreed to lay down their arms.

Blackfish led his captives north. One night, as a test of courage, he forced Daniel to run the gauntlet. The Shawnee stood in two long lines armed with clubs, sticks, and tomahawks. Daniel ran a zigzag path that evaded many of the blows. A stumble could have meant his death. At the end of the line, a warrior stepped in front of him, tomahawk raised. Daniel put his head down and rammed the man in the chest. Blackfish was so impressed, he later adopted Daniel.

At Fort Detroit, Blackfish introduced Daniel as his new son. Daniel showed Governor Hamilton his British militia commission. Then he hinted that the Kentucky settlers were loyal to King George. The lie may have fooled the British. Blackfish, however, already was planning a new attack on Boonesborough.

It was June before the Shawnee relaxed their guard. When they did, Daniel made his escape. After he shook off pursuit, he headed for Boonesborough. Four days and 160 miles later, he stood in front of the gates. In his Shawnee dress, no one knew him at first. Even his looks had changed. Blackfish had plucked out his hair, leaving only a topknot.

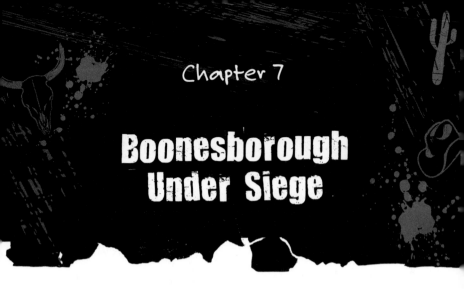

Chapter 7

Boonesborough Under Siege

O nly Jemima rushed to welcome her father when Daniel returned to Boonesborough. Rebecca had taken the other children back to North Carolina. She thought her husband was dead. Daniel set that problem aside and turned to the task of fighting the Shawnee. Under his command, the men strengthened the fort's defenses. The women stockpiled food and bandages. Outside the stockade, a crew cleared the brush. Riflemen needed a clear field of fire.

The work stopped on September 7, 1778. A unit of British militia troops from Canada had appeared outside Boonesborough. With them were Blackfish and four hundred Shawnee.

Blackfish called on the fort to surrender. In return, he promised safe passage to Detroit. Wary of promises, the men in the fort voted to fight.

Daniel and Squire relayed the message to Blackfish. They also gave him false reports on the fort's strength. To support the deception, the women dressed like men and carried rifles.

The talks dragged on. On September 11, 1778, Blackfish offered a peace treaty. After both sides signed, Daniel reached to shake the chief's hand. Suddenly, Blackfish grabbed his arm and tried to drag him away. As the men struggled, both sides opened fire. In the confusion, Daniel managed to make a mad dash to safety.

For two days, each side blazed away. Then the siege force tried a new tactic. Blackfish put his braves to work on a tunnel. If it worked, the tunnel would undermine the fort's walls. While the digging went on, the Shawnee set cabin roofs ablaze with fire arrows.

At that dark moment it started to rain. The downpour did more than put out the fires. The rain-soaked earth caved in the tunnel. With that, the Shawnee broke the siege and slipped away. The settlers rejoiced in their triumph. They later claimed to have killed thirty-seven Shawnee, while losing only two of their own.

Daniel did not have much time to savor the victory. A few hotheads still blamed him for the surrender of the salt boilers. Now they added the charge of treason.

A Shawnee raiding party exchanges gunfire with Boonesborough's defenders during the siege of 1778.

Boone had been too friendly with the British, they said. In October, Daniel stood trial at a court-martial.

His only option was to sidetrack the Shawnee, Daniel told the court. If he had failed, the fort would have fallen. Women and children would have been massacred. When he escaped, he pointed out, he went back to the fort. There he stayed, to be "tomahawked and shot . . . and to risk his very life to save them." The court found him not guilty. It also promoted him to the rank of major.

A year later, Daniel brought his family back to Kentucky. He settled Rebecca and the children at Boone's Station, five miles north of Boonesborough. That winter, Daniel went to Virginia to buy more land for himself and some friends. In James City, thieves stole $20,000 from his saddlebags. Once again, he had lost everything.

Daniel worked hard to earn back the stolen money. He served as sheriff of Fayette County and as a deputy surveyor. In April 1781, his neighbors sent him to serve in the Virginia Assembly. At Charlottesville, he was captured and then released by British troops. In October, the British surrendered at Yorktown. The fighting in the East was over.

The war on the frontier lasted longer. In August 1782, Daniel helped turn back the Shawnee in the Battle of Blue Licks. The victory was dearly won. His son Israel died in his arms during the battle.

A final skirmish with the Shawnee had a happier ending. In 1783, Daniel was hanging tobacco to dry in a small shed. As he climbed up the drying racks, four Shawnee burst in. "Now, Boone, we got you. You no get away more," one of them called.

Daniel was not one to panic. He smiled and chatted with his "old friends," all the while gathering an armload of dried tobacco. When the braves were off guard, he threw the tobacco in their faces. As he had hoped, the dust blinded the Shawnee. Daniel had time to slip out of the shed and run to safety.

Chapter 8

Civilization Closes In

In 1783, Daniel was nearing his fiftieth birthday. If he was hoping to live a quiet life, those hopes were soon blasted. A sheriff came to Boone's Station to tell Daniel that he would have to move. His land, the court had ruled, belonged to someone else.

Dismayed but not daunted, Daniel moved his family to Limestone, Kentucky. Settlers traveling by flatboat entered Kentucky through the tiny settlement on the Ohio River. Limestone "is become a grate Landing place," Daniel noted. Before long, the Boones owned a wharf, a warehouse, a store, and a tavern. Travelers ate Rebecca's meals and slept in a back room of the tavern.

During the next three years, Daniel made more than a hundred surveys. Clients paid him with pieces of the land that he surveyed. Following the custom of the day, Daniel described boundaries in terms of landmarks, such as trees and streams. When he finished a survey, Daniel promised clear title to the land. Then, more woodsman than lawyer, he often failed to do all the paperwork. When the courts took their land away, some of his clients sued Daniel.

In 1784, a backwoods teacher named John Filson published a history of Kentucky. Only a brief final section, "The Adventures of Colonel Daniel Boon," caught the public eye. The thirty-four pages were based on Filson's talks with Daniel. Popular in America, the book was a sensation in Europe. No one seemed to care that the story was full of tall tales. What did Daniel think? Perhaps he had a twinkle in his eye when he said, "All true! . . . Not a lie in it!"

Authors and painters featured Daniel in their works. On paper, it appeared that the new hero was a rich man. He had some one hundred thousand acres under claim. He owned a business and three slaves. He was in demand as a surveyor. His land titles, however, were in dispute. Land sharks took him to court. They contested his right to thousands of acres. Some of his business ventures failed. His name sold books, but no one paid him a share of the profits.

As Daniel Boone grew older, his joints and muscles ached, the result of living an adventurous outdoor life. Despite the pain, he remained an avid hunter.

After just six years at Limestone, Daniel moved upstream to Point Pleasant. He opened a store there. Customers seldom found him behind the counter. Surveying, guiding new-comers, and selling horses filled his days. But he was happiest when he went hunting and trapping. His friends, he found, still trusted him. They sent him east to serve a second term in the Virginia Assembly. The state put him in command of the local militia.

In 1792, the United States welcomed Kentucky as its fifteenth state. The new state now needed merchants and farmers, not woodsmen. By this time, Daniel was feeling the weight of his years. His joints and muscles ached. He still loved to hunt, but now Rebecca traveled with him to keep camp.

In 1795, the Boones moved thirty miles west to Brushy Fork. Daniel and his youngest son, Nathan, built a one-room cabin. Four of his married daughters lived nearby.

Legal judgments were trickling in. By 1789, Daniel had lost most of his land. In the fall, a sheriff came to arrest him for failing to appear in court. The lawman went home empty-handed. Daniel had given up his land claims and moved far upriver. He told his children that "he would rather be poor than retain an acre of land . . . so long as claims and debts hung over him."

Out west, Spain needed settlers to farm the empty land that would one day be called Missouri. Daniel accepted Governor Zenon Trudeau's offer of 850 acres. The Spanish official knew that where Daniel went, others would follow. Daniel and Rebecca headed west in 1799. They brought with them a flock of sons, daughters, and grandchildren. Daniel walked every step of the seven hundred miles.

The Boones settled in the Femme Osage District near the Missouri River. In June 1800, Daniel was appointed to new duties as one of Missouri's first syndics. A syndic served as sheriff, judge, and jury all in one. Daniel held court under a tall elm known as the Judgment Tree. No one ever appealed his decisions.

Chapter 9

A Most Uncommon Man

In 1800, Spain ceded the Louisiana Territory to France. Three years later, France sold Louisiana to the United States. The transfer left all Missouri land claims in doubt. To hold his land, Daniel should have been living on it and farming it. Busy with his duties, he had done neither. To keep the family close, he and Rebecca had lived on a son's land.

The Spanish, Daniel argued, had excused syndics from the rules. The laws of the United States, however, did not recognize Spanish customs. An American land commission denied his claim. The courts backed the commission. In 1810, at age seventy-five, Daniel found himself landless and nearly broke.

That same year, Daniel asked Congress to restore his 8,500 acres of land. Kentucky's senators did their best, but Congress was slow to act. Two years passed before Daniel's land was finally restored. Even then,

An act for the relief of Daniel Boone

Be It enacted by the Senate and house of Representatives of the united States of America in Congress assembled

that Daniel Boone be and he is hereby confirmed in his title to 1000 arpens of land claimed by him by virtue of a concession made to him under the Spanish government bearing date the 28th day of January 1798

and It shall be the duty of the Recorder of land titles for the Territory of Missouri

to Issue to the said Daniel Boone or to his heirs a certificate in the same manner and of the same description, as the said Daniel Boone would have been entitled to receive If his claim to the said land had been confirmed by the Commissioners appointed for the purpose of ascertaining the rights of persons claiming land in the Territory of Louisiana, or by the Recorder of land titles for the said Territory of Missouri —

In 1810, Daniel Boone sent a petition to the U.S. Senate requesting the return of 8,500 acres that a land commission had taken from him. After a long delay the Senate granted his petition—but gave him only 850 acres.

he was short-changed. Congress awarded him only 850 acres, just a tenth of what he claimed.

The War of 1812 renewed the struggle between the United States and Great Britain. Daniel volunteered, certain that his knowledge of frontier warfare would be needed. The army, however, turned him down.

By that time, Daniel was grieving over the death of his wife. Rebecca died in 1813 at age seventy-four. A granddaughter said he had suffered "the Saddest affliction of his life." Even the return of his 850 acres gave Daniel little cheer. The news brought old creditors out to press their bills. Daniel paid the claims by selling the land. "I have paid all my debts," he told his family. "No one will say when I am gone, 'Boone was a dishonest man.'"

Old age did not rob Daniel of his love of the outdoors. He made his last long hunt sometime around 1810. On that expedition, Daniel hunted and trapped along Wyoming's Yellowstone River. Back home, he complained that Missouri was filling up. He talked about heading west, perhaps to California.

As the years passed, the old woodsman contented himself with smaller joys. He sang to his grandchildren and told them stories. Shawnee friends came by to visit. He repaired rifles, carved powder horns, and

Daniel Boone's legend continued to grow after his death. His adventurous life has been dramatized in books, movies, and on television. This 1936 poster drew moviegoers to the action-packed film, *Daniel Boone*.

sewed moccasins. His mind was still sharp. A visitor asked him if he had ever been lost. "No, I was never lost," Daniel shot back. "But I was bewildered once for three days."

His death came on September 26, 1820, after a brief illness. The crowd that came to the funeral overflowed Jemima's house. Services had to be held out back in the barn. Ever since Rebecca's death, Daniel had kept his coffin ready. His family used it to bury him beside her.

In 1845, Kentucky had a change of heart. The state that had driven him out now wanted him back. Daniel and Rebecca were reburied at Frankfurt, Kentucky. They lie there today beneath a marble monument.

The legends about Daniel have grown taller than his monument. Books and films have credited him with superhuman feats. If the great pioneer were alive today, he would set the record straight. "Many heroic . . . adventures are related of me which exist only in the regions of fancy," Daniel once told a visitor. "With me the world has taken great liberties, and yet I have been but a common man."

No one who knows the true story would agree. Daniel Boone was one of this nation's most *uncommon* men.

Glossary

ambush—A sudden attack made from a concealed position.

assembly—The lower chamber of a state legislature.

buckskins—Pants and jackets made from the tanned hide of a male deer.

canebrake—A dense thicket made up of reeds or bamboo.

commission—A government document that appoints someone to a particular rank or office.

Continental Congress—The legislative body that governed the newly independent colonies until 1789.

court-martial—A court that tries officers and enlisted personnel who have been accused of crimes under military law.

flatboat—A raftlike boat with a cabin on the deck.

flintlock—A firearm that uses a flint embedded in the hammer to produce a spark. The spark, in turn, ignites a powder charge and fires the weapon.

frontier—A region just being opened to settlers.

gauntlet—Men armed with sticks or other weapons arrange themselves in two facing ranks and try to hit the person forced to run between them. Running the gauntlet can be a form of punishment or a test of courage.

legend—A story that many people believe, but which is often untrue in whole or in part.

militia—Part-time soldiers who are called to duty in times of emergency.

moccasins—The soft leather shoes often worn by American Indians.

pioneers—The men and women who open a wilderness area to settlement.

pound (£)—The British monetary unit.

powder horn—A cow horn used for carrying gunpowder.

salt lick—A natural salt deposit that animals come from miles around to lick.

siege—An attack on a town or fortress that traps the defenders within their fortified defenses.

speculator—Someone who engages in risky ventures in hopes of making a quick profit.

stockade—An enclosed area walled with sharpened stakes.

surveyor—Someone who determines the boundaries of a plot of land by measuring angles and distances from known landmarks.

tomahawk—A light, short-handled ax used as a weapon by many American Indian tribes.

trail signs—The traces left by humans and animals as they move through a wilderness area.

treason—The act of betraying one's country by giving aid to its enemies.

Further Reading

Books

Brown, John Mason. *Daniel Boone: The Opening of the Wilderness.* New York: Sterling Publishing Co., 2007.

Harness, Cheryl. *The Trailblazing Life of Daniel Boone: And How Early Americans Took to the Road.* Washington, D.C.: National Geographic, 2007.

Ransom, Candice. *Daniel Boone.* Minneapolis, Minn.: Lerner Publications, 2005.

Salas, Laura Purdie. *The Wilderness Road, 1775.* Mankato, Minn.: Bridgestone Books, 2003.

Zronik, John. *Daniel Boone: Woodsman of Kentucky.* New York: Crabtree Publishing Co., 2006.

Internet Addresses

The Adventures of Daniel Boone: Archiving Early America
<http://www.earlyamerica.com/lives/boone/>

Daniel Boone Homestead
<http://www.danielboonehomestead.org/>

Daniel Boone Wilderness Trail
<http://www.danielboonetrail.com/>

Index